The Relaxation Solution

Also by Stephen Diamond

The Relaxation Solution Workbook and Journal

The Relaxation Solution

The Secret to Stress-Free Living

By Stephen Diamond

Empty
Mind

Publishing

Published by Empty Mind Publishing LLC
Tucson, AZ 85748
emptymindpublishing.com

This book details the author's personal experiences with and opinions about stress relief. The author is not your healthcare provider, and this book is not intended as a substitute for the medical advice of psychologists or physicians. Individual results vary. You should consult a physician in matters relating to your health and particularly with respect to any symptoms that may require diagnosis or medical attention.

Library of Congress Control Number: 2022938703
ISBN 979-8-9862949-0-2

Publisher's Cataloging-in-Publication Data

Names: Diamond, Stephen Martin, 1947- author.
Title: The relaxation solution : the secret to stress-free living / Stephen Diamond.
Description: Tucson, AZ : Empty Mind Publishing, 2022. | Series: Relaxation solution, bk. 1.
Identifiers: LCCN 2022938703 (print) | ISBN 979-8-9862949-0-2 (trade paperback) | ISBN 979-8-9862949-1-9 (ebook : epub) | ISBN 979-8-9862949-2-6 (ebook : Kindle) | ISBN 979-8-9862949-3-3 (audiobook)
Subjects: LCSH: Mindfulness (Psychology) | Meditation. | Self-actualization (Psychology) | Self-help techniques. | Stress management. | BISAC: SELF-HELP / Self-Management / Stress Management. | SELF-HELP / Meditations. | HEALTH & FITNESS / Alternative Therapies.
Classification: LCC BF637.M56 D53 2022 (print) | LCC BF637.M56 (ebook) | DDC 158.1/3—dc23.

Contents

List of Exercises

Dedication

To my mother, whose untimely death revealed to me the insidious relationship between stress and disease.

Your memory is a blessing.

Epigraph

It's very important that we re-learn the art of resting and relaxing. Not only does it help prevent the onset of many illnesses that develop through chronic tension and worrying; it allows us to clear our minds, focus, and find creative solutions to problems.

—Thích Nhất Hạnh

Introduction

The car was out of control. Veering and spinning across the highway, it didn't respond to the steering wheel or the brakes. It was only going to stop when it ran into some immovable object.

I realized in that moment that there was nothing I could do to influence the outcome. I was entirely powerless.

And in that moment of recognition something wonderful happened. I became entirely calm, entirely still. I knew there was nothing I could do, so I was free from any pressure to do anything. All I had to do was watch and wait.

Time slowed. My perceptions became sharp and vivid. I was curious but not concerned about what was happening, unworried about what the next moment would bring. My mind was clear and open.

Afterward, I thought *Why isn't my experience always like this? What exactly made me feel so free? Is it possible to feel this free all the time?* And I set out to find the answer.

You may never have had such a dramatic experience, but I'm willing to bet you've had a taste of what I'm talking about.

Have you ever been "in the zone" when playing sports or video games? That same sense of clarity and flow is what I felt.

Have you ever gotten lost in the beauty and wonder of a sunset, a mountain scene, a seascape? That same sense of freedom from care is what I felt.

Have you ever gotten so involved in an intricate bit of craft work or art work that you lost track of everything else, "lost yourself in your work"? That same sense of focused presence is what I felt.

Have you ever been so carried away watching a movie, listening to music, or reading a book, that you feel afterward like you've been taken away from yourself on a journey? That's also what I'm talking about.

All these states of mind are reminders that we are naturally free, that tension and worry are artificial discomforts we impose on ourselves because we've never been properly taught how to relax, how to go with the flow, how to be focused without being uptight.

What have I discovered? Those are skills we can learn. In this little book I'll show you how to start freeing yourself from the tyranny of tension. Let's get started.

Oh, you'd like to know about my car? Well, after spinning once and flipping onto its side, it did find an immovable object: a lamppost. The car was totaled. I and my passenger were shaken up but uninjured. Then I was arrested and jailed overnight.

But that's a story for another time.

How to Use This Book

This is primarily a book of exercises, not physical but mental exercises. You'll want to perform the exercises, ideally on a regular basis. I've given some Sample Schedules at the back of the book.

The exercises are guided meditations and visualizations derived from my years of teaching mindfulness for stress reduction. I'll say a bit more about them in the section What Is The Relaxation Solution?

The point is that the Tension Problem (see Chapter One) is very real. Each of us has been acquiring tension every day of our lives, and we continue to acquire it. Reading about it and gaining insight into the process may help a little, but to truly solve the problem and free ourselves from unnecessary tension requires more. It requires discovering our own built-in Relaxation Solution. These exercises will gently and naturally lead you there.

Audio Files for Streaming or Download

Many of the exercises in the book are done with the eyes closed. It's much easier and more effective to listen to the instructions during the exercise rather than trying to remember them. I've recorded them all for your exclusive use. You have permission to stream and/or download these on your smartphone, tablet, computer, or other device, for your own personal use. You'll find a list of links to the audio files in the Audio Recordings section at the back of the book and a reminder before each exercise.

Who Am I?

My name is Steve Diamond. I go by the more formal *Stephen* on the book cover, but in real life I'm simply Steve.

I've been teaching stress reduction in person and online since 2013, and studying it for a lot longer. I've taught one-on-one and in groups. I've taught free classes at public libraries and done expensive private coaching.

This book gives you a concise, easy-to-follow program containing what my clients and students have found most helpful. If you follow, I trust that you will find it helpful too.

HOWEVER, I want you to hear this loud and clear:

Don't believe a word I say!

That's right. Don't believe anything I tell you when I'm explaining how things work or how things are. I'm not here to tell you how your mind works. That's for you to discover. I'm here to provide some tools to help you explore your own immediate experience and make those discoveries for yourself.

I'll make some suggestions along the way about what you may be finding as you use those tools. Don't take the suggestions overly seriously. They're just guideposts. If they help you in your explorations, great. If what I say doesn't make sense to you, or if what you find within yourself is different than what I say, **believe in your own experience**. I can't emphasize this enough.

In other words, do the exercises and draw your own conclusions.

It doesn't do you a lot of good to hear about or read about your mind. That's where many self-help books fail. All they do is try to tell you about you. But you're the ultimate authority on you. So, don't believe anything I tell you...**unless you've verified it for yourself.**

Chapter One: The Tension Problem

Tension is a habit. Relaxing is a habit. Bad habits can be broken, good habits formed.
—William James

All Stress All the Time

We're surrounded by things that stress us out. Rarely do most of us get any relief from incessant noise, news, advertising, and pressure to get things done—in our jobs, in our relationships, and at home. It can feel like we're constantly bombarded with stressful situations. They're almost impossible to avoid.

Even when we manage to get away for a night out with friends, a weekend with the family, a few hours out in nature, or just a few minutes relaxing in a warm bath, it's hard to avoid the long reach of the world that assaults us through our mobile devices, TVs, and radios.

We respond to all this stress by creating tension. We create tension in our bodies and tension in our minds. And all this tension is making us ill. It's literally killing us.

Why do we make ourselves tense in response to stress? The short answer is that we learned to do it to protect ourselves, but it got out of hand and became an unhelpful habit. Imagine someone is about to punch you in the gut. What do you do? You tense your gut muscles, of course. That tension will protect you when the blow lands. An extreme example is a circus strongman who can deflect a cannonball to the abdomen by tensing those muscles.

This defensive response works well in those particular situations where we see what's coming and we know that tension will protect us. But what evolved as a useful mechanism against physical threats doesn't work well when most of the threats we face nowadays are mental. We aren't likely to encounter a saber-tooth cat in the street. We're very likely to encounter a demand from our boss or from a bill collector, in which cases tension is not our friend.

So we've learned without realizing it to make ourselves tense when it's not going to do us any good. In fact, it harms us. Stress from a variety of causes—social isolation, depression, unemployment, anxiety attacks, to name a few—can alter our bodies. Stress actually accelerates the aging of our cells in measurable ways that are associated with chronic disease and premature aging. (See Science References at the back of the book for some of the science about this.)

How we respond to these stressors makes all the difference. Do we let them get to us? Or can we remain calm and relaxed in the midst of the storm?

That's what this book is all about: how to relax. How to relax truly, profoundly, naturally, and effortlessly. How to relax at a level rarely experienced in this modern world.

It's about discovering our own innate Relaxation Solution. Everyone has it. Finding it is only a matter of a simple shift in perspective. This book will guide you there.

Chapter Two: The New Mindfulness

That the birds of worry and care fly over your head, this you cannot change, but that they build nests in your hair, this you can prevent.
—Chinese Proverb

My story, continued

After the car accident (see Introduction) I began looking for ways to free myself from the tyranny of tension. I read a lot, including topics in Eastern and Western philosophy, self-help, psychology, and more.

Having no other option, I experimented on myself. I tried to apply each theory that seemed as if it might be helpful, and I looked for results. Each time I was disappointed. (You may be thinking this sounds familiar. Good! There's hope, I promise.)

Then, some years ago, I had the opportunity to train as a Mindfulness teacher. This meant I could continue to explore new methods, and I could now get feedback from others. I wasn't limited to my own experience. Between Mindfulness and all my previous studies, I had all the tools to succeed.

What you're reading here is the result of my research, of all my trial and error. It starts with discovering a new approach that I call the New Mindfulness.

What is the New Mindfulness?

First, a few words about the old Mindfulness. As I practiced according to what I'd been taught, I found there were definite benefits. I was more relaxed. I didn't take stressful situations or thoughts as seriously.

But there was also something missing. It felt unnatural. It felt as if I was forcing myself to change rather than removing obstacles and letting change happen. I had to take one more step. I had to find a new approach.

What I found was the New Mindfulness.

In a nutshell, where the old Mindfulness is forced, the New Mindfulness is relaxed. Where the old Mindfulness tries to impose practices and patterns, the New Mindfulness allows change to emerge spontaneously and naturally.

I'm not going to explain the differences philosophically or theoretically. That wouldn't be very helpful. Instead, I'm going to lead you through exercises that let you discover the New Mindfulness for yourself.

What is The Relaxation Solution?

The Relaxation Solution is a new way of seeing, a new perspective on how we respond to stress. It's a recognition that we've learned to respond to stress by creating tension in our bodies, in our minds, and in our emotions. We do it to ourselves without knowing it. We actually make efforts that create tension, and we often aren't aware that we're doing it.

Once we become aware, we can stop. It's as simple as that. But as long as we remain unaware of what we're doing to ourselves, we'll never find true relaxation.

This book contains a set of effortless, natural exercises proven to bring freedom from the tyranny of tension by leading you to discover the Relaxation Solution for yourself. All you have to do is follow along.

Here's an example. Not just an example, but an all-important first step. I call this **Exercise 0** because it's the foundation of the entire Relaxation Solution. It couldn't be simpler. There's no recorded audio for this one because it's so simple you'll have no trouble remembering what to do when your eyes are closed.

Exercise 0: Understanding Tension

With your eyes open, hold one hand up in front of your chest and make a fist. If it's more comfortable, you can grasp a pen, pencil, small rock, or something similar. Or just use your bare hand.

Concentrate on making a tight fist. Not so tight that you injure yourself, just tight enough that you feel the effort going into clenching your fist. Feel the effort, that's the key. Feel the effort, and now begin to notice the sensation of tension in the fist. The effort and the tension are two separate, distinct happenings. You deliberately apply effort, and tension comes about as a result.

Now let go of the effort. Stop clenching your fist. Let your hand drop.

If you were watching the tension sensation as you stopped the effort, you noticed that the tension disappeared as soon as you removed the effort. Do it again. Clench your fist, noticing the effort and the tension as separate things. Watching the sensation of tension, stop the effort. Notice how the tension vanishes.

Now close your eyes and repeat the exercise. Without the distraction of vision, it's easier to notice the difference between the effort and the tension. Repeat several times, until you feel you see this clearly. Then open your eyes.

Now direct your attention to a part of the body where you've noticed excess tension before. Maybe it's the shoulders and back of the neck. Most of us tend to hold tension there. You could also look at the jaw muscles and the muscles around the eyes.

Look very closely at any tension you find, remembering how it felt to clench and relax your fist. Look closely, and you'll discover that you're actually making a subtle effort, unconsciously, outside your foreground awareness. For example, if there's tension in your shoulders, you're probably shrugging them a little, pulling them toward your ears.

Close your eyes and look again if you're having trouble seeing this with them open.

Once you see the effort, you can just stop, as you did when you relaxed your fist. Just stop, and the tension disappears.

When you don't see the effort, the tension persists. Once you see it, you're in control. You can stop the effort because it's no longer hidden from your awareness.

Conclusions of Exercise 0

What have you seen? First, that tension arises primarily as a sensation in the body. Second, that tension is a result of effort, and when the effort is removed the tension disappears. In our everyday lives, the effort is often unconscious. It's often outside our foreground awareness. Once we learn to become aware of it, we're in control. We're able to stop.

This discovery about physical tension in the body isn't completely new. You've probably heard it said, "If you feel tension in your shoulders, intensify it, make it tighter, and then let it go." This advice comes up in yoga and other stress relief programs.

Now you know why that advice works. It works because it makes you aware of the effort you're already exerting, by asking you to intensify it. But no one tells you that's why it works. That insight is missing. You aren't told that you're already making the effort that causes the tension. You aren't told that the effort and the tension are two separate experiences. Now you've discovered it for yourself.

You also aren't told that it also applies to your mental life, your emotional life, and your spiritual life. That's where this approach is unique.

These discoveries are the bedrock of the Relaxation Solution. They will sustain you in extending it to your body, mind, and spirit. I encourage you to return to this section of the book as often as necessary to reinforce the insights. I'll remind you to repeat Exercise 0 frequently.

About The Exercises

When I say that all you have to do is follow along with the exercises, I don't just mean read. You have to actually do the exercises, and do them regularly, if you want to experience the Relaxation Solution for yourself. I've laid out a sample schedule at the back of the book, and I've included a worksheet to help you keep track.

Many of these exercises are guided meditations that I've developed over the years. Some are variations on meditations used in Mindfulness and other programs. I've modified them in line with the insights of the New Mindfulness. Others are original for this program.

Please don't be put off by the word *meditation*. I'm not going to ask you to sit in an uncomfortable posture for hours at a time. And if you've meditated before, this isn't the same. **If meditation hasn't worked for you in the past,**

you'll be pleasantly surprised by what you'll find in this program.

About Meditation

First let's clear up some misconceptions about meditation. You may have run across some of these ideas. You may even have come to believe them. Now you can let them go.

1. *Meditation will quiet my mind. If my thoughts don't stop, I've failed.*

   No. This is unrealistic and unnecessary. With the Relaxation Solution, you're going to discover a new relationship with thoughts. That's what you need for peace of mind. You don't need to stop them.

2. *Meditation will transport me to a different state of consciousness, something like a psychedelic drug. If it doesn't, I've failed.*

   Again, no. Ordinary consciousness is truly everything we need. Special states exist, but they're always temporary. We're looking for something that doesn't come and go.

3. *Meditation requires special equipment and special postures.*

   It doesn't. You can sit comfortably in a chair, on a cushion, on a bench. You can even lie down (as long as you stay awake). Whatever works for you is perfectly fine.

4. ***Meditation means I have to concentrate on a thing or an image.***
   Not so. Some kinds of meditation are like this, but we won't be doing any of them.

5. ***Meditation won't work unless I do it for hours at a time.***
   Sorry, no. I promise not to subject you to anything like that!

6. ***Meditation takes a lot of effort. It's hard work.***
   Really, no. In the Relaxation Solution, meditation is easy, gentle, and very relaxing.

Herding Cats

Another few words about point number 6. The keyword for the entire Relaxation Solution is *gentle*. When doing the exercises, and as we go about our daily lives, we want to remember to be gentle with ourselves.

In the meditations we're often working with the attention. We're noticing what it is that we're paying attention to, and we're very gently influencing our attention.

If we try too hard, it's like herding cats. They scatter. It's hopeless.

When we're gentle, it's like playing with one little kitten. When the kitten starts to wander, we gently and lovingly divert it. Or we pick it up with infinite care and bring it back home.

That's how we treat ourselves, gently and lovingly.

If the image of a kitten doesn't work for you, think of a baby. Sometimes it wants to settle down, and sometimes it wants to crawl away and explore. We always treat it lovingly and gently, no matter what it does. That's how we treat ourselves.

Exercise 1: Watching the Breath

Meditation on the breath has been around for thousands of years. This version, updated for the New Mindfulness, will give you a sound basis for reaping the benefits of the Relaxation Solution: freedom from tension and stress in the body, in the mind, in the emotions, in your entire way of being.

Be sure to see How to Use This Book to learn about the free audio files you can stream or download for all the exercises in the book. Like the others, the link for this one is in the Audio Recordings section.

Before you begin, repeat Exercise 0, relaxing the clenched fist. This will remind you that tension results from effort and relaxation results from stopping the effort.

Now find a place where you won't be disturbed. Set aside 10-15 minutes for this exercise. Less is okay. More is okay.

But I recommend 10-15 minutes. Set a timer if you like, or put a clock where you can glance at it occasionally.

[Audio begins here.] Sit comfortably. Find a posture that feels dignified and also lets you relax. Let your eyes close.

Take a deep breath. Let it out with a sigh. Once more, a deep breath and a sigh. Now breathe normally, without trying to influence your breathing in any way.

Notice that you can feel the body breathing. You can feel the sensation of the abdomen and chest expanding and contracting as you inhale and exhale. Gently place your attention there, centered in the abdomen.

You aren't trying to concentrate; you're just giving your attention a place to rest. You aren't trying to exclude anything else that's going on (like sounds, thoughts, images); you're just centering your attention on the abdomen as it expands and contracts.

You may notice a tendency to think about your breathing. That's okay but unnecessary. You may notice a tendency to control your breathing. That's also okay and also unnecessary. The body already knows how to breathe. You're just watching.

You'll certainly notice other things going on: sounds, thoughts, mental images, other sensations—a whole kaleidoscope of things. It's quite all right. Let them happen. Let them be. Let them come and go like clouds drift-ing across the sky.

Sometimes these other things will distract you from watching the breath. That's all right too. It happens to ev-eryone. Whenever you notice that it's happened, just re-member, 'Oh, I intended to keep watching my breath' and you'll find your attention returns gently to the breathing sensations in the abdomen.

Sometimes the distractions will be very quick, momentary, and you'll return right away to the breath. Other times you'll get lost in thought for minutes at a time before you notice. That's okay. It doesn't mean you're bad at this. It just means you're beginning to notice how the mind works.

Continue until the end of the time you've set aside. Then gently let your eyes open. *[Audio ends.]*

Conclusions of Exercise 1

You've discovered that your attention is observable. You have the ability to know what you're paying attention to. This may seem simple and obvious or it may not. For some people seeing it for the first time is a revelation. In either case, this seeing is important. It will help you discover the Relaxation Solution.

Chapter Three: The Body

Pain is a relatively objective, physical phenomenon; suffering is our psychological resistance to what happens. Events may create physical pain, but they do not in themselves create suffering. Resistance creates suffering. Stress happens when your mind resists what is... The only problem in your life is your mind's resistance to life as it unfolds.

—Dan Millman

What is the body?

This sounds like a ridiculous question, doesn't it? Isn't the answer obvious?

What is the body? Why, it's me.

What is the body? Why, it's what I see when I look in the mirror or at a photograph.

What is the body? Why, it's this thing right here that I feel when something touches it.

What is the body? Why, it's my skin and everything inside it.

Yes, but what is the body *really*? Is it a collection of organs? Is it a collection of cells? Of molecules? Of atoms? Of elementary particles?

Let's try another way. Here's an exercise.

Exercise 2: What Is the Body?

See How to Use This Book to learn about the free audio files you can stream or download for all the exercises in the book. Like the others, the link for this one is in the Audio Recordings section.

[Audio begins here.] Sit comfortably. Find a posture that feels dignified and also lets you relax. Close your eyes and visualize your body. Notice what comes to mind. Is it what you see when you look down? Is it the image you see in the

mirror? Is it an image from a photograph? Maybe it's more abstract and general, like an image from an anatomy text-book.

Whatever the image, realize that you're seeing it in your mind's eye based on a *memory*. As long as your eyes are closed, the body isn't appearing to your sense of sight at all. If you're picturing it, you're remembering something you saw in the past.

Now let the visualization go and bring to the foreground of your attention the sensations that represent the body. Notice the sensations of pressure where your feet rest on the floor, your rear and your back rest on the chair. Notice the texture sensations of your clothes on your skin and any moving air on your skin. Also notice internal sensations, like maybe a pain in your big toe or in your neck. Also notice breathing sensations: the air as it flows in and out of your nostrils; the muscles of the chest and abdomen as they expand and contract.

Realize that with your eyes closed this group of body sensations is the only immediate knowledge you have of your body. Everything else, everything you visualized, everything you thought you knew about the body, was no more than memory or something you've been told. Your immediate experience of the body is nothing more or less than a group of sensations.

Keep your eyes closed and sit with this knowledge for a few moments. Then open your eyes. *[Audio ends.]*

Conclusions of Exercise 2

What have you discovered? Most everything you thought you knew about the body was either memory of things you've seen in the mirror, in photographs, by looking down, or it was hearsay, that is, something you've been told in class or in a book about what constitutes the body. The only immediate knowledge you could find was a group of sensations. Those sensations constitute your direct knowledge of the body.

Tension in the body: how to release it

Now that you've discovered, in your immediate experience, what the body is and what it isn't, let's take a closer look.

First we want to perceive and understand where tension comes from, how it comes to be. Once we see this clearly, we'll be well on our way to knowing how to release and relax unwanted tension. That skill will be the basis for dramatic transformation in your well-being, physically, emotionally, and spiritually. This is the foundation, and it's remarkably simple.

Exercise 3: Creating and Releasing Tension

This is a repeat of Exercise 0, the fist clench, with added insights. Recall Exercise 2 as you clench and relax your fist. See that you perceive the tension the same way you perceive anything in the body: as a sensation.

Now let go of the effort. Stop clenching your fist. Let your hand drop.

If you were watching the tension sensation as you stopped the effort, you noticed that the tension disappeared as soon as you removed the effort. Do it again. Clench your fist, noticing the effort and the tension as separate things. Watching the sensation of tension, stop the effort. Notice how the tension vanishes.

Now close your eyes and repeat the exercise. Without the distraction of vision, it's easier to notice the difference between the effort and the tension. Repeat several times, until you feel you see this clearly. Then open your eyes.

Conclusions of Exercise 3

What have you seen? First, that tension arises primarily as a sensation in the body. It belongs to the group of sensations you discovered earlier (Exercise 2). Second, that tension is a result of effort, and when the effort is removed the tension disappears.

These discoveries are the keys to unlocking the Relaxation Solution for body, mind, and spirit. Feel free to return to this section of the book as often as necessary to reinforce the insights.

Exercise 4: Releasing Tension throughout the Body

See How to Use This Book to learn about the free audio files you can stream or download for all the exercises in the book. Like the others, the link for this one is in the Audio Recordings section.

[Audio begins here.] Sit comfortably. Find a posture that feels dignified and also lets you relax. Let your eyes close.

Take a moment to recall Exercise 2, where you discovered the group of sensations representing the body. Let those sensations come to the foreground of attention.

Now you're going to scan the entire group of body sensations. Remembering the lesson of Exercise 3, clenching the fist, you'll create and release tension in each part of the body. This time you'll be gentle in your effort. You don't have to create as much tension as you did when clenching the fist. A small effort will do fine, just enough so you can feel some tension in each body part. This is called leaning in, leaning into the effort, leaning into the tension.

As you visit each area, watch to see whether or not there's any tension before applying effort, and watch to see whether the area feels more relaxed after removing the effort.

Begin by directing attention to the right foot, the toes of the right foot. Are they already tense? Gently curl the toes or press them into the floor. Hold, feeling that the effort is creating the tension. Then release.

Now visit the rest of the right foot and ankle. Gently tense the muscles. Hold. And release.

Now the right lower leg. Gently tense the calf muscle. Lean in. Feel the effort and the tension. Hold. Release.

Now go to the right upper leg, the large muscles at the front and back of the right thigh, and the right buttock. Tense them with a gentle effort. Hold and release.

Now repeat on the left side. Go to the left foot, the toes of the left foot. Gently curl the toes or press them into the floor. Hold, feeling the effort and the tension. Then release.

Now visit the rest of the left foot and ankle. Gently tense the muscles. Lean in. Hold. And release.

Now the left lower leg. Gently tense the calf muscle. Feel the effort and the tension. Hold. Release.

Now go to the left upper leg, the large muscles at the front and back of the left thigh, and the left buttock. Tense them gently. Lean in. Hold and release.

Now find the abdomen. Gently tense the muscles circling the abdomen: front, sides, and lower back. Hold and re-lease.

Now move the attention to the chest, the muscles at the front and sides of the chest, and the upper back. Gently tense, hold, and release.

Now visit the right hand, starting with the fingers. Gently tense the fingers of the right hand, hold, and release.

Now scan the rest of the right hand, tensing the muscles of the palm, leaning in, holding, and releasing.

Now the right forearm. Flex the wrist slightly to help locate the forearm muscle sensations. Gently tense, hold, and release.

Now going to the right upper arm, the biceps and triceps. Gently tense those muscles. Hold. Release.

Now visit the left hand. Gently tense the fingers, hold, and release.

Now the rest of the left hand, gently tensing the muscles of the palm, holding, and releasing.

Now the left forearm. Flex the wrist slightly to help locate the forearm muscle sensations. Gently tense, hold, and release.

Now going to the left upper arm, the biceps and triceps. Gently tense those muscles. Hold. Release.

Now direct the attention to the shoulders and back of the neck. This is an area where many of us habitually hold tension without realizing that we're doing it to ourselves. You're going to see how that works.

Notice if there's already tension in the area. If there is, notice how it's arising. Are you doing it?

Now gently tense the shoulder and neck muscles by shrugging the shoulders and pulling the head back. Lean in. Feel that the effort is creating tension. Now let go of the effort and watch the tension dissolve. Repeat. Feel that your shoulders and neck are more relaxed than they were.

You'll notice throughout the day that your attention returns to this area, and you'll remember that your habitual tension is created by your own effort. Each time this happens, you'll find it easier to stop the effort and release the tension.

Now find the muscles around the mouth, the jaw and the lips. Gently tense, hold, and release.

Now scrunch up your whole face, including the cheeks, around the eyes, and the forehead. Hold the effort, feel the tension, and release.

Now feel the muscles of the scalp, at the top and back of the head. Gently tense, hold, and release.

Now visualize the entire body filled with a warm, relaxing glow. Starting with the top of the head, picture and feel that a warm radiance is cascading down throughout the body, from the head through the neck, the shoulders, down both arms to the fingertips, through the chest, the back, the abdomen, the pelvis, and through both legs all the way to the toes.

Feel the warm, soothing radiance embracing the whole body. Take a few moments to enjoy this relaxing sensation.

When you're ready, let the eyes open gently. *[Audio ends.]*

Conclusions of Exercise 4

You've discovered that you can consciously release tension in the body. First, by watching closely, you see that you're actually creating the tension in the first place by unconsciously exerting effort. Next, by bringing awareness and exaggerating this process, you found that you can release the effort and feel the tension disappear.

Once you've practiced this full-body version of Exercise 4 a few times, I invite you to invent your own mini-scan versions that visit parts of the body where you often notice tension. You don't have to sit and do them formally. You can use these mini-scans anytime and anywhere:

- Sitting at your desk or in a meeting

- Waiting in line

- Driving (just remember to keep your eyes open!)

- Lying in bed, trying to sleep

- Any time you feel tense

The more often you do this, the more often you'll remember naturally and spontaneously to do it. You won't have to try to remember. When there's tension in your shoulders, for example, you'll notice it and you'll say to yourself 'Oh, yeah. I'm creating that tension by tightening those muscles.' And you'll stop. You'll stop making the effort that creates the tension, and the tension will disappear.

This is your essential foundation in the Relaxation Solution as it applies to your body. You're about to discover that everything you've learned about how it works in the body also applies to other facets of your being: your emotions, your thoughts, and yes, even your spirit.

Chapter Four: Emotions

If you are distressed by anything external, the pain is not due to the thing itself but to your own estimate of it; and this you have the power to revoke at any moment.
—Marcus Aurelius

Interlude

I couldn't see. Someone was screaming.

It had always been like this. Someone was screaming in the dark. It would always be like this.

Someone was screaming. It was dark. I couldn't see.

Then something changed. It wasn't completely dark. The black was gradually becoming gray.

Someone was screaming in the featureless gray.

Then sensations happened. *Oh, the pain! The pain in my belly! White hot! Terrible!*

Someone was screaming.

Oh, the white hot pain!

Someone was screaming, and I noticed it was me.

I stopped screaming. My belly still hurt, but I saw that I didn't have to keep screaming about it. When I noticed I was the one screaming, I was able to stop.

I opened my eyes. I saw I was in a hospital ward. I remembered.

I just had my appendix out. They said they would cut me open and they did. It feels like the surgeon left a scalpel behind in my belly. It will pass. I can relax.

What is an emotion?

This sounds like another silly question, doesn't it? Surprisingly, it seems to have no single authoritative answer. Here are a few that I found:

What is an emotion?

- A biological state

- A psychological state

- A strong feeling

- A conscious mental reaction

- A complex experience of consciousness

Let's see if we can discover for ourselves, by exploring our own immediate experience, what makes up an emotion.

Exercise 5: Finding an Emotion

See How to Use This Book to learn about the free audio files you can stream or download for all the exercises in the book. Like the others, the link for this one is in the Audio Recordings section.

[Audio begins here.] Sit comfortably. Find a posture that feels dignified and also lets you relax. Let your eyes close.

Take a deep breath. Let it out slowly. And another.

Let the body sensations come to the foreground. Quickly scan from head to toe, looking for any tense spots. When you find one, amplify the tension a little, lean into it. Then let it go, let it relax.

Now let the body sensations recede into the background. Engage your imagination. Call to mind and visualize a situation where you were angry. Picture it as clearly and vividly as you can. It doesn't matter if it's hazy and dim. Just picture it as clearly as you can.

Let the incident play out in your imagination. What do you see? What do you hear? What do you smell and taste?

Who is present? What are they saying? How are you responding?

Feel yourself getting angry. Amplify the things that are making you angry. Feel yourself getting angrier. Really feel angry.

Now, bring the body sensations back to the foreground while still visualizing the incident. Notice what sensations are present in the body as you get angry.

What are the sensations in your face? Are you frowning? Tensing your forehead and around the eyes? Tensing your jaw, lips, and tongue? Does your face feel hot?

What are the sensations in your neck and shoulders? Is there movement? Is there tension? Is there a hollow or nauseated sensation in the throat?

What are the sensations in your chest? Does it feel as if your heart is racing? Is there tension? Is there heat?

What are the sensations in your abdomen? Does it feel hot? Tense? Sick?

Now stop visualizing the situation. Let the incident go while the body sensations remain.

You still feel angry. Scan the body again to see what sensations make up this feeling. Scan the face, neck, shoulders, chest, and abdomen.

Realize that without the visualized incident, there's nothing more or less to feeling angry than this particular combination of sensations. This is revelatory.

Recalling Exercise 4, lean into each area, one by one, and let go of the effort that's creating tension there. Let go of the effort in the face, the neck, the shoulders, the chest, and the abdomen. Watch as the tension disappears.

When you find something other than tension, lean into that too. Does your face feel hot? Lean into it by picturing the heat intensifying and expanding like a balloon. Then pop the balloon and allow cool air to flow in.

Does your abdomen feel unsettled and sick? Lean into it by gently centering your attention there. Then picture an opening, a window in the abdomen. Let the sick feeling escape through the window and dissipate.

When you feel you've come to the end of your exploration, sit quietly for a moment, then gently let the eyes open. *[Audio ends.]*

Conclusions of Exercise 5

You've discovered that your emotions exist primarily as body sensations. Just like with muscle tension, you now know how to gently lean into the emotion sensations and then let them go, let them flow away, let them escape.

Feel free to be playful with this exercise. Repeat it with different scenarios and different emotions. Invent your own images, metaphors, and visualizations. Maybe an uncomfortable feeling turns to smoke, passes through your skin, and floats away. Maybe it shrinks to become so tiny that it emerges through a pore like a bead of sweat and then evaporates. There are no wrong ways to do this.

Chapter Five: The Mind

The truth is that stress doesn't come from your boss, your kids, your spouse, traffic jams, health challenges, or other circumstances. It comes from your thoughts about these circumstances.
—Andrew J. Bernstein

What is the mind?

I promise this will be the last silly question. This one seems to be harder to pin down than the first two ("What is the body?" "What is an emotion?"). It certainly takes more words to explain. Here are a few examples:

- "the element of a person that enables them to be aware of the world and their experiences, to think, and to feel; the faculty of consciousness and thought." - Oxford Language

- "the element or complex of elements in an individual that feels, perceives, thinks, wills, and especially reasons," - Merriam-Webster

- "**Mind** refers to the aspects of intellect and consciousness manifested as combinations of thought, perception, memory, emotion, will and imagination, including all of the brain's conscious and unconscious cognitive processes. 'Mind' is often used to refer especially to the thought processes of reason." - Psychology Wiki

- "mind, in the Western tradition, the complex of faculties involved in perceiving, remembering, considering, evaluating, and deciding. Mind is in some sense reflected in such occurrences as sensations, perceptions, emotions, memory, desires, various types of reasoning, motives, choices, traits of personality, and the unconscious." - Britannica

Does it really have to be that complicated? Let's take it for granted that we have an intuitive idea of what we mean by mind. For our purposes I propose a much simpler way to put it: Mind is our inner life.

Tension in the mind: how to release it

Following our overall theme, we expect to find that tension in the mind is created by effort and can be released by stopping the effort. Let's see how we can verify that in our own immediate experience.

Exercise 6: Tensing the Mind

First we'll use a simple example to clarify what it feels like to make a mental effort. Start by reminding yourself what it feels like to make a physical effort. Refer to Exercise 0, the clenched fist, for a reminder of the details if you like. Hold your hand out, clench it into a fist, and release. See how the effort causes the tension in the hand, and see how when you stop the effort, the tension disappears.

Now we're going to repeat another familiar exercise, but with a twist. This is a variation on Exercise 1, watching the breath.

Remember to see How to Use This Book to learn about the free audio files you can stream or download for all the exercises in the book. Like the others, the link for this one is in the Audio Recordings section.

[Audio begins here.] Sit comfortably. Find a posture that feels dignified and also lets you relax. Let your eyes close.

Take a deep breath. Let it out with a sigh. Once more, a deep breath and a sigh. Now breathe normally, without trying to influence your breathing in any way.

Notice that you can feel the body breathing. You can feel the sensation of the abdomen and chest expanding and contracting as you inhale and exhale. Gently place your attention there, centered in the abdomen. You've done this before. You've given your attention a place to rest.

Here's the twist. As you watch the breath, try very hard to do nothing but that, nothing but watching the breath. Clench your mind, clench your attention around the breath the way you clenched your hand into a fist.

Don't overthink this. It doesn't matter if you're not sure how to do it. Just try hard to force your attention to focus on the breath. Try hard to clench your mind around the breath.

While you're doing that, notice what it feels like. You'll see that this effort is no different from the effort component in clenching your fist. If that isn't apparent, clench and release the fist several times, keeping your eyes closed. Look closely enough so you separate the effort and tension components. If that isn't so clear to you with the fist, try tens-ing and releasing your shoulders. See how the effort is dis-tinct from the tension.

Now return to clenching the attention around the breath. Make the effort to keep the attention there, to prevent it from wandering. Keep clenching the mind for a few sec-onds. Then let it go. Stop the effort. Stop trying to control your attention. Stop trying to do anything.

What do you notice? Take a moment to look and see. Re-peat the mental clenching and the letting go as many times as you like. Pause the audio if you want. Notice deeply what the letting go feels like.

Now return once again to tensing the mind, to clenching your attention around the breath. This time notice more about what the tension feels like. Look closely. What are you feeling as you create this tension? Look for uncomfort-able sensations similar to what you found in Exercise 5 when you were experiencing anger. Maybe there's a simi-lar sense of queasiness in the stomach or gut. Whatever it is, whatever you find, lean into it.

Now release the effort to force the attention onto the breath, and simply lean into the sensation. If it doesn't dissipate on its own, visualize an opening that lets it es-cape from your body, just as you did in Exercise 5. Picture the discomfort flowing away. Take as long as you need. Pause the audio if you like.

Now return to tensing the mind. Return to forcing your attention to stay on the breath. Look again for an associated feeling, an uncomfortable sensation. You may notice a different one, or the same one may reappear. In either case, repeat what you did before:

Release the concentration effort. Lean into the sensation. See if it dissipates. If not, visualize a way for it to escape, and let it go.

You can repeat this as many or as few times as you like. When you feel it's enough, or when your allotted time is done, gently open your eyes. *[Audio ends]*

Conclusions of Exercise 6

This one has been a little different. You've discovered that when you stop clenching the mind, the resulting tension doesn't always resolve on its own. Sometimes it does, and sometimes you must do something extra, a visualization, to let it go.

You've uncovered an important relationship. You've seen that mental effort does indeed create mental tension, just as physical effort creates physical tension. You've also seen that once you identify these mental knots, you can find ways of relaxing them.

In Chapter 6, we'll explore how to carry all these insights into everyday life.

Chapter Six: Putting It Together

Breathe. Let go. And remind yourself that this very moment is the only one you know you have for sure.

—Oprah Winfrey

The Relaxation Solution in Everyday Life

If you've stuck with me this far, you've made important discoveries that will help keep stress from causing you grief and messing up your life. But how (you're wondering) do you take them from sitting still into the hustle and bustle of everyday living? How do you put them to work?

Here's the best advice I can offer: **Find ways to help you remember to let go.**

This has two parts.

Trust the Process

The exercises are key. Remember how I said earlier that if you want the benefit, you actually have to do the exercises regularly? I wasn't kidding. Here's why.

When you do them regularly, you form new habits that eventually persist. I talked in Chapter One about the habit we've learned of responding to stress with tension. The exercises open the door to see that habit in action, and they reveal that once we see, we can let go of that learned response. That's how the exercises help to break old habits and establish new ones.

It doesn't happen overnight. It can't. We've spent years, decades, creating and reinforcing the old habits. They won't simply vanish. Reading about them, gaining some understanding and insight, is a good first step. But for most of us it's not enough. We have to repeatedly perform the new ways or they won't stick.

It doesn't have to be every day, but it does have to be regular. I recommend doing one or more of the exercises at least twice a week for a few minutes, longer if you like.

At some point you'll see the magic begin to happen. You'll see at times during your day that you notice tension and you respond by letting it go. I call it "magic" because it simply seems to happen, with no apparent cause. You'll be walking along or sitting at your desk, you'll find yourself noticing tension in your shoulders, and you'll naturally let it go. Simple as that. And then you'll remember, 'Oh, I've been doing those exercises from *The Relaxation Solution*. I knew this was going to happen!'

So that's one way. Trust the process, and you won't even have to find ways to remember to let go of tension. Those moments of noticing and remembering will naturally and effortlessly come about, almost by magic.

Create Your Own Reminders

Here's where you can get creative and playful. Find places in your physical and mental landscapes where you can change something and jolt yourself out of your habitual mindset into remembering.

Here are some examples for your physical environment. Prepare yourself so when you notice these objects you respond by remembering to look for tension and let it go. Make it fun!

- Move your toothbrush (or other commonly used object) to the other side of the bathroom sink. When you get used to the new location, move it back.

- Change the unlock setting on your smartphone. When you get used to the new one, change it again.

- Get a sheet of adhesive stickers (dinosaurs, birds, flowers, whatever you like). Stick them in places you're bound to notice, like the bathroom mirror, refrigerator door, car dashboard. When you get used to them, move them and change them.

- If you're driving, remind yourself before setting out that whenever you see a red light you'll stop to look for tension while you're stopping the car. When you get used to that, change it from red lights to red cars.

Here are some examples for your mental landscape. This may be a little trickier. You can't just move things around. What you can do is train yourself by repeating for a few seconds each day an affirmation like 'When I notice *X* I'll remember to look for tension and release it.'

- When you notice you've acquired an earworm (repeated song or tune).

- When you notice you're mentally cursing out someone or something.

- When you notice negative self-talk, like 'I'm a failure.'

- When you notice you've gotten lost in thought, telling yourself a story.

Adding these deliberate reminders to your toolkit will augment the automatic benefits you'll get from repeating the exercises.

Chapter Seven: Awareness

Within you, there is a stillness and a sanctuary to which you can retreat at any time and be yourself.
—Hermann Hesse

How and where is this all happening?

Up to this point I've been speaking from a perspective that's primarily psychological. That's where most of the literature on stress relief—and most of the literature on self-help in general—begins and ends. I'm not criticizing that. It's an appropriate and helpful perspective. But there's a bit more I'd like to say from a different point of view, a perspective that's more about spirit.

How would you respond if I were to ask, "What's your true home? Where do you dwell? What territory do you inhabit?"

Off the top of our heads, most of us would answer simply with their address and their nation. Or, as James Joyce's schoolboy protagonist in *A Portrait of the Artist as a Young Man* gave it:

> Stephen Dedalus
> Class of Elements
> Clongowes Wood College
> Sallins
> County Kildare
> Ireland
> Europe
> The World
> The Universe

What does immediate experience have to say? We've been relying on immediate experience in our explorations so far. Let's take it one step further.

Consider this. Does immediate experience include knowing any of the objects on Stephen Dedalus's list?

My name. I know my name. You do, but how do you know it? Your parents or guardians told you. Everyone calls you by it. If they call you something different, you think they've made a mistake. But do you really know your name? It's all hearsay, right? Someone told you. When you look into immediate experience for who and what you are, your name isn't there. In the here and now, it's no more than a memory. It isn't imprinted in your mind as a necessary feature. It's just something you remember frequently.

Okay, then my address. I know where I live. Look again. It's the same as your name, isn't it? Someone told you. You see it on a sign. You remember and use it frequently. Others use it to find you. But it's not present in immediate experience other than as a memory.

We could do the same with each element in Stephen's list. None of them is immediate. They're all hearsay, all memories. None of them can be verified in immediate experience.

So, what can we verify?

One thing we can always verify beyond any shadow of doubt is that we are present. We are aware. We can't even conceive of seriously saying "I am not present" or "I am not aware," because we know we would have to be present and aware to say so. This we know with certainty.

Now, where do we truly live? Let's find out!

Exercise 7: Resting In Awareness

See How to Use This Book to learn about the free audio files you can stream or download for all the exercises in the book. Like the others, the link for this one is in the Audio Recordings section.

Find a place where you won't be disturbed. Set aside at least 15 minutes.

[Audio begins here.] Sit comfortably. Find a posture that feels dignified and also lets you relax. Let your eyes close.

Notice what happens as your eyes close and the visual world disappears. You relax automatically because a significant source of tension has just been removed: You're no longer constructing the world of visual objects. Yes. Open and close your eyes again to verify for yourself. When your eyes are open, you see yourself surrounded by solid objects that your mind is constantly constructing from visual sense impressions. When your eyes are closed, your mind is profoundly relieved because it doesn't have to do all that work anymore. Open and close them again. See? We're paring down distractions to get at the core of immediate experience.

For most of us, vision is the dominant sense. When we close our eyes hearing takes over. Let's explore the imme-diate experience of the world as it appears to the sense of hearing.

Let sound be in the foreground of experience. What sounds do you notice? If you're playing the audio, there's the sound of my voice. What else? Fans, machinery, traffic, voices, music?

Where are the sounds appearing? With your eyes closed, you have some memories indicating where some sounds originate. You think those voices are outside the window because you saw some kids playing out there earlier. You think the traffic must be from the main road down the block.

But, just as with the items on Stephen Dedalus's list, you have no immediate experience of those locations. They're nothing more than memories. All you have now is sound. All you have now is hearing.

And where is hearing? What does the hearing world feel like?

You noticed when your eyes closed that the objects, bor-ders, and boundaries of the visual world disappeared. The walls are gone. The floor is gone. The ceiling is gone. The sense of enclosed space is gone.

What remains? Feel your way into the hearing world. Explore it. Do you find any borders or boundaries? Does anything prevent this world from being limitless? Can you imagine being outside of it looking in?

No. What you sense in this exploration is a clear, open, borderless, limitless spaciousness. It may seem to be centered where you are and expand endlessly in all directions. Or it may seem that you **are** this clear spaciousness.

You are tasting your real home. You are seeing that you are present **as** this open clarity in which all the particular facets of experience take place. All the sounds, all the sensations, all the thoughts, all the feelings—they all come and go in this borderless openness that is your aware presence.

Watch any of these objects as they appear, remain awhile, and subside. Watch a thought go by, a sound, a body sensation. They're the same in that they're all appearing to your aware presence.

Like space itself, your presence is always open and receptive to any object appearing. Whether it's a thought, a sight, or a sound, there's never any resistance. Resistance may arise a moment later as a reaction, but the object is already there without resistance, otherwise the resistance couldn't happen. This entire play, this entire drama, is appearing in and as your aware presence. This is your real home. You inhabit it fully at every moment.

Now take a deep breath, release it, let all these details go, and simply allow experience to be exactly as it is this very moment. Don't look for particular objects, don't try to influence your attention in any way. Simply watch as experience unfolds in your presence.

Enjoy the spaciousness. Enjoy the peace. Enjoy the total relaxation of having let go of every expectation, every rule, every belief. Just be the experience.

Just be.

When you're ready, allow your eyes to open. *[Audio ends.]*

Conclusions of Exercise 7

What you've discovered is deeply intimate. It's your very nature, the source of all peace and tranquility. I can't tell you how to conceptualize it. You may want to write about it in a journal. You may want to simply contemplate it.

In any case, I encourage you to return to resting in awareness as often as you like. You needn't go through all the preliminaries each time. Just close your eyes and allow experience to unfold exactly as it is. Enjoy the clear spaciousness. Enjoy the unshakable knowledge that you are always present as this awareness, without boundaries, utterly un-stressed, utterly relaxed.

For me, this is the answer to the quest I began in the Intro-duction, the search for flow, the key to being in the zone. This deep well of peace and tranquility that is our aware presence is always available. It's always available because it's inseparable from ourselves. In essence it is what we are, our constant, uninterrupted experience.

Chapter Eight: Next Steps

The illiterate of the 21st century will not be those who cannot read or write; they will be those who cannot learn, unlearn, and relearn.
—Alvin Toffler

Where to go from here?

That's entirely up to you.

If you've read through the book without doing the exercises, I urge you to go back and try them. They aren't difficult or painful, and they're the best way I know to break the harmful habit of making yourself tense in response to stress. Reading about the habit and understanding it aren't enough. Only repetition will break old habits and establish new ones.

Take a look at the Sample Schedule in the back of the book. You can use it as is or rip it up and make your own. If you really want your tension level to change, set a schedule, stick to it as best you can, and keep track in an Exercise Log. There's a simple model log at the back of the book. And consider getting the companion volume, *The Relaxation Solution Workbook and Journal*. It has a page for each day plus weekly check-ins and monthly self-evaluations. Keep track, and you'll avoid fooling yourself about what you're really doing.

Beyond that, I would really like to hear from you. Let me know if you liked the book or hated it, if you have questions or comments, if there are specific topics you'd like me to cover in future volumes. My contact information is in the section **Was This Book Helpful?** after the next chapter, along with a final request. Thank you.

Chapter Nine: Lovingkindness (Metta)

Metta sees truly that our integrity is inviolate, no matter what our life situation may be. We do not need to fear anything. We are whole: our deepest happiness is intrinsic to the nature of our minds, and it is not damaged through uncertainty and change.
—Sharon Salzberg

Opening the Heart

I'd like to conclude this little book the same as I conclude many of my Mindfulness classes, with a *metta* (lovingkindness) meditation. This offers an antidote or a balancing factor to all the mental work we've been doing up to this point. Metta opens the heart. It lights up our heart center, radiating peace and love to the world and to ourselves.

The practice of metta probably began in India before the time of the Buddha (circa 500 BCE). References can be found in Buddhist, Hindu, Jain, and other texts, where compassion, benevolence, and lovingkindness are considered important virtues.

According to the Pali Canon, Buddha recommended it to his followers, saying:

> *No other thing do I know, O monks, on account of which unarisen ill will does not arise and arisen ill will is abandoned so much as on account of this: the liberation of the heart by benevolence. For one who attends properly to the liberation of the heart by benevolence, unarisen ill will does not arise and arisen ill will is abandoned.*

and

> *One sleeps easily, wakes easily, dreams no evil dreams. One is dear to human beings, dear to non-human beings. The devas protect one. Nei-*

ther fire, poison, nor weapons can touch one. One's mind gains concentration quickly. One's complexion is bright. One dies unconfused.

This is not to say that metta is a particularly Buddhist or religious practice. You can think of it as a secular prayer for the world and its inhabitants. You can think of it as a way to open your own heart to compassion and love. You'll be correct in either case.

My version of metta meditation is a little different from the classical formulation. I truly hope it brings you joy and peace.

Exercise 8: Metta Meditation

Remember to see How to Use This Book to learn about the free audio files you can stream or download for all the exercises in the book. Like the others, the link for this one is in the Audio Recordings section.

[Audio begins here.] Sit comfortably. Find a posture that feels dignified and also lets you relax. Let your eyes close.

Take a moment to become accustomed to the openness and clarity of the world when the eyes are closed. Let your breath settle down.

Now imagine you're in a large room. It could be a reception hall, theater lobby, train station, large living room—whatever comes to mind. Perhaps many people are present, perhaps just a few.

Bring to mind someone you love without reservation. It could be your spouse, child, parent, sibling, dear friend. It could be a beloved pet. They might be currently in your life or not.

Visualize catching sight of them across the room. Imagine and notice how you feel. Your face relaxes into a smile. Your eyes glow. You feel the heart center in your chest warming and expanding.

Drop your attention into the heart center, into the chest. Feel that you are the heart; the heart is you. Feel yourself brightening, warming, and expanding to embrace the beloved individual across the room. Imagine them coming closer. As you walk toward each other, your heart is full. Your loving embrace is complete and unconditional. Picture the embrace when you reach each other. Feel the love that envelops you both, and say to yourself:

May they be safe. May they be happy. May they be free. May they be loved.

May they be safe from harm. May they be truly happy. May they be free from suffering. May they be loved.

Now change the visualization to center on yourself as a person, with all your strengths and weaknesses, all your quirks and flaws, all your humanity. Picture yourself in your own loving embrace, and say to yourself:

May I be safe. May I be happy. May I be free. May I be loved.

May I be safe from harm. May I be truly happy. May I be free from suffering. May I be loved.

Now bring to mind a small community of family and friends, people for whom you feel warmth and affection. Picture them each as a distinct personality. See them all enclosed in the glowing warmth of your heart's embrace, and say to yourself:

May they be safe. May they be happy. May they be free. May they be loved.

May they be safe from harm. May they be truly happy. May they be free from suffering. May they be loved.

Now bring to mind a group of acquaintances about whom you feel neutral. Maybe they're people you see only occa-sionally and aren't close to. Picture them all enclosed and embraced in your glowing heart center, and say to your-self:

May they be safe. May they be happy. May they be free. May they be loved.

May they be safe from harm. May they be truly happy. May they be free from suffering. May they be loved.

Now think of someone you actively dislike. Bring to mind the reasons for your disliking them. Let those reasons be present while you invite the individual into your loving embrace, into the warmth of your heart center. Picture this clearly and vividly, and say to yourself:

May they be safe. May they be happy. May they be free. May they be loved.

May they be safe from harm. May they be truly happy. May they be free from suffering. May they be loved.

Now let go of picturing that individual, and imagine your loving presence expanding to embrace the whole world, the world we inhabit that often seems to need healing, to need our love. Notice how easily the world fits into the un-limited spaciousness of your loving embrace. Picture all the people in all the world, in all their billions, known and unknown, and say to yourself:

May they be safe. May they be happy. May they be free. May they be loved.

May they be safe from harm. May they be truly happy. May they be free from suffering. May they be loved.

And now let yourself, your heart, your loving presence, ex-pand without limit, expand to embrace the solar system, the galaxy, all the galaxies in all the universe. Picture all the conscious beings, known and unknown, in all the worlds of all the stars of all the galaxies, and say to your-self:

May all beings be safe. May all beings be happy. May all beings be free. May all beings be loved.

May all beings be safe from harm. May all beings be truly happy. May all beings be free from suffering of any kind. May all beings be loved.

Sit quietly for a moment, enjoying the warmth and the peace. When ready, let your eyes open. *[Audio ends.]*

Was This Book Helpful?

Thank you very much for reading my book, for staying with it to the end. I know there are a lot of other things you could have done with your time. I hope you've found the investment worthwhile, and I thank you for taking a chance on trusting me to guide you. I feel the responsibility keenly. I've done my very best to adhere to the truest principles I've been able to discover.

If you have found value here, may I ask a small favor? If you could take a few moments to leave a short review on your favorite online retailer or book review site, I would appreciate it so much. It will encourage me to write more and it will encourage others to take a chance on my work. You can find all the retail links here: **r.elax.in/7eea**. It's also on Goodreads at **r.elax.in/aj1a** and on BookBub at **r.elax.in/fjj3**.

I plan to add to the Relaxation Solution series. If you want to be notified of early-bird discounts, previews, and exclusives on my advanced courses and other materials, you can sign up here: **r.elax.in/news**.

I'd also love to hear from you directly. If you have a question or a topic you'd like me to cover, you can email me at **stephen@stephendiamond.me**.

Thank you.

Bonuses

Booklet: *The Tension Problem*

I invite you to get my free booklet, *The Tension Problem (and how to solve it)*. It includes a stress self-evaluation quiz as well as an introduction to the Tension Problem and the Relaxation Solution. You can download it here: **r.elax.in/tense**.

Discounts and Special Offers

For early-bird announcements, previews, and exclusive discounts on my advanced courses and other materials, sign up here: **r.elax.in/news**.

Audio Recordings

I've recorded the exercises for your convenience. You have permission to stream and/or download each of the exercise audios for your own personal use. Each one is listed here with a shortened URL you can type and a QR code you can scan.

Exercise 1: Watching the Breath
r.elax.in/sound1

Exercise 2: What Is the Body?
r.elax.in/sound2

Exercise 4: Releasing Tension throughout the Body
r.elax.in/sound4

Exercise 5: Finding an Emotion
r.elax.in/sound5

Exercise 6: Tensing the Mind
r.elax.in/sound6

Exercise 7: Resting in Awareness
r.elax.in/sound7

Exercise 8: Metta Meditation
r.elax.in/sound8

Sample Schedule

These are suggestions, not prescriptions. Use them or make up your own!

Week One

- Monday: Exercise 0, Exercise 1
- Tuesday: Exercise 2, Exercise 3, Exercise 4
- Wednesday: Exercise 5
- Thursday: Exercise 0, Exercise 1
- Friday: Exercise 0, Exercise 6
- Saturday: Exercise 2, Exercise 3, Exercise 4
- Sunday: rest, or your preference

Week Two and Beyond

- Monday: Exercise 0, Exercise 6
- Tuesday: Exercise 2, Exercise 3, Exercise 4
- Wednesday: Exercise 5, Exercise 8
- Thursday: Exercise 7
- Friday: Exercise 0, Exercise 6
- Saturday: Exercise 2, Exercise 3, Exercise 4
- Sunday: Exercise 7, Exercise 8

Exercise Log

Copy this page, or make your own. For a more immersive and focused experience, I strongly suggest that you get the companion volume, *The Relaxation Solution Workbook and Journal*. It has a page for each day plus weekly check-ins and monthly self-evaluations.

Day/ Date	Time	Exercise	Duration	Notes

Science References

Studies Linking Stress & Mortality

(type the short URLs following the titles into a web browser)

- Heavy stress and lifestyle can predict how long we live—**r.elax.in/fv4t**
  National Institute for Health and Welfare via Science Daily, March 11, 2020

  " Life expectancy is influenced not only by the traditional lifestyle-related risk factors but also by factors related to a person's quality of life, such as heavy stress... Being under heavy stress shortens their life expectancy by 2.8 years.

- High Stress Levels Result in Higher Mortality Rates —**r.elax.in/t8d7**
  Journal of Aging Research via HCPLive, October 25, 2011

  " If you didn't know it already, you do now: stress kills. That's according to the results of a new study that concludes that men who experience persistently moderate or high levels of stressful life events over a number of years have a 50% higher mortality rate.

- Emotional Distress Can Speed Up Cellular Aging—
  r.elax.in/yjju
  Psychology Today, April 7, 2014

  " A wide range of studies has shown that the
  stress caused by things like untreated depression, social isolation, long-term unemployment, and anxiety attacks can speed-up the
  aging process by shortening the length of each
  DNA strand.

- The interaction between stress and positive affect
  in predicting mortality—**r.elax.in/vk5x**
  Journal of Psychosomatic Research via ScienceDirect,
  September, 2017

  " Stress-related disease emerges...out of the fact
  that we so often activate a physiological system
  that has evolved for responding to acute physical emergencies, but we turn it on for months
  on end, worrying about mortgages, relationships, and promotions.

- Why Zebras Don't Get Ulcers—**r.elax.in/ks5e**
  1994 book by Robert M. Sapolsky, Stanford University
  biologist

  " Stress-related disease emerges...out of the fact
  that we so often activate a physiological system
  that has evolved for responding to acute physical emergencies, but we turn it on for months
  on end, worrying about mortgages, relationships, and promotions. Don't miss out!

Acknowledgments

Great thanks to my mentors, students, beta readers, and all who have helped me to hone these ideas in conversations and online discussions. You know who you are.

Credits

Cover art © by Alina Osadchenko, licensed by Dreamstime.com.

Cover design by Stephen Diamond.

Guided meditation sound recordings voiced by Stephen Diamond, copyright © 2022 by Stephen Diamond.

About the Author

Stephen Diamond has studied and practiced mindfulness, meditation, self-realization, and nonduality for 50 years. He founded More Than Mindful in 2015 and launched The Relaxation Solution program in 2022.

A former singer, software architect, and political candidate, Steve began teaching mindfulness in 2015. He has taught public and private classes, coached private clients, and presented at gatherings large and small. His guided meditations have been played nearly 30,000 times on the Insight Timer mobile app, where users have rated them 4.6 out of 5.

Steve is deeply familiar with various nonduality teachings, including Zen Buddhism and Advaita Vedanta. And he's practiced several types of meditation: TM (transcendental meditation), zazen, vipassana, metta, and mindfulness meditation.

In 2022 he brought all that experience plus new techniques and insights into his ground-breaking stress relief program, The Relaxation Solution.

Read more at Stephen Diamond's site: **r.elax.in/sdme**.